ENGINEERING WONDERS OF THE 21ST CENTURY



# Great TRAIN Designs

BY SOPHIE WASHBURNE

Cavendish Square
NEW YORK

Published in 2023 by Cavendish Square Publishing, LLC
29 East 21st Street, New York, NY 10010



Website: cavendishsq.com



Cataloging-in-Publication Data
Names: Washburne, Sophie.
Title: Great train designs / Sophie Washburne.
Description: New York : Cavendish Square, 2023. | Series: Engineering wonders of the 21st century | Includes glossary and index.
Identifiers: ISBN 9781502665218 (pbk.) | ISBN 9781502665225 (library bound) | ISBN 9781502665232 (ebook)
Subjects: LCSH: Railroad trains--Juvenile literature. | Railroad trains--Design and construction--Juvenile literature. | Railroad trains--History--Juvenile literature.
Classification: LCC TF148.W37 2023 | DDC 385'.22--dc23

Editor: Jennifer Lombardo
Copyeditor: Michelle Denton
Designer: Rachel Rising

The photographs in this book are used by permission and through the courtesy of: Cover Ortodox/Shutterstock.com; cover, pp. 1–48 (gears) Artistdesign29/Shutterstock.com; cover, pp.1–48 (grid) Cesar Termulo Jr/Shutterstock.com; cover, pp. 1–48 (boxes) Olessia_Art/Shutterstock.com; p. 4 https://commons.wikimedia.org/wiki/Ensor Mill - steam engine - geograph.org.uk - 2572893.jpg p. 6 Historic Collection/Alamy Stock Photo; p. 7 https://commons.wikimedia.org/wiki/File:Coalbrookdale_loco.jpg; p. 8 Kasix/Shutterstock.com; p. 10 https://commons.wikimedia.org/wiki/File:Transcontinental_railroad_route2.png; p. 11 Ivy Close Images/Alamy Stock Photo; p. 12 Sergey Merkulov/Shutterstock.com; p. 16 Science History Images/Alamy Stock Photo; p. 18 Joshua Woroniecki/Shutterstock.com; p. 20 https://commons.wikimedia.org/wiki/File:ROBERT-DAVIDSON-NEW-PICTURE-DavidsonColour-taken-in-1870s-1-743x1152.jpg; p.23 Matyas Rehak/Shutterstock.com; p. 24 Tabi24/Shutterstock.com; p. 26 cyo bo/Shutterstock.com; p. 28 TTphoto/Shutterstock.com; p. 30 Martin Harvey/Alamy Stock Photo; p. 33 dbtravel/Alamy Stock Photo; p. 34 Claudio Divizia/Shutterstock.com; p. 36 GE_4530/Shutterstock.com; p. 38 inxti/Shutterstock.com; p.41 Naeblys/Alamy Stock Photo; p. 43 Janus Orlov/Shutterstock.com.



CPSIA compliance information: Batch #CSCSQ23: For further information contact Cavendish Square Publishing LLC, New York, New York, at 1-877-980-4450.

Printed in the United States of America

# CONTENTS

# Introduction

Throughout most of history, travel has taken a very long time. Even going from one town to another could take several days when the only forms of transportation available were walking or horseback. Boats and carriages could help cut down travel time, but they could also be expensive. For many years,

Early steam engines such as this one were huge and could not be moved. Before being used for transportation, they powered factories.

only the wealthy could afford to take vacations. Poorer people generally traveled only when they needed to.

The invention of the steam engine was one of the first steps toward making travel faster and more affordable. Ships were fitted with this kind of engine, and suddenly they were making record time across the ocean. A sailing ship could take up to two months to cross the Atlantic Ocean, but early steamships cut that trip down to about two weeks. People loved this new, faster travel. Not only could they get places quickly, but they could also send goods around the world. They wanted the same convenience for overland travel.

The idea of creating a set path for a vehicle on land was not new. Beginning around 600 BCE, the ancient Greeks carved grooves into granite rocks specifically to transport goods over land. They designed wheels to fit inside the grooves and added the wheels to wooden carts pulled by horses. In 1550, the Germans created something similar, called wagonways. They laid wooden rails down over dirt roads to make it easier for horses to pull chains of wooden-wheeled wagons. In the 1700s, the wooden rails and wheels were replaced with iron, which stood up to heavy use better.

These systems paved the way for train travel as we know it in modern times. Horses pulled the earliest trains because

Shown here is an early wagonway.

the steam engines that existed in the 1700s were huge and could not be moved. Changes to the early designs had to be made so steam engines could be moved. They had to be smaller and lighter but still powerful enough to pull heavy loads. New designs led to the use of steam to power both ships and trains.

In the late 1700s, James Watt invented a steam engine that used less fuel and was lighter. This inspired Richard Trevithick of Wales to design the first steam locomotive, or vehicle that moves train cars, in 1804. His locomotive pulled 70 men and 10 tons (9 metric tons) of iron nearly 10 miles (16 kilometers) at 5 miles (8 km) per hour. This marked the real beginning of mechanized train travel.

This engraving shows Richard Trevithick's locomotive design.

The flanges on train wheels such as this one help keep the train on its track.

CHAPTER ONE

# Making Improvements

Even though Trevithick carried passengers on his first trip, the main purpose of trains during this time was to carry freight, or goods. Engineers worked to improve everything from brakes to train rails. They studied how to hook many cars together safely using a joint called a coupling. Solutions to these problems resulted in **flanged wheels,** new track rail designs, and imaginative ways of building up soil.

## GETTING FROM HERE TO THERE

In the 1800s, trains were the best way to transport people and things long distances over land. Engineers figured out how to build strong wooden boxes on the wheeled cart frames. These became known as freight cars. Later, these freight cars were made from iron and steel to carry even heavier loads.

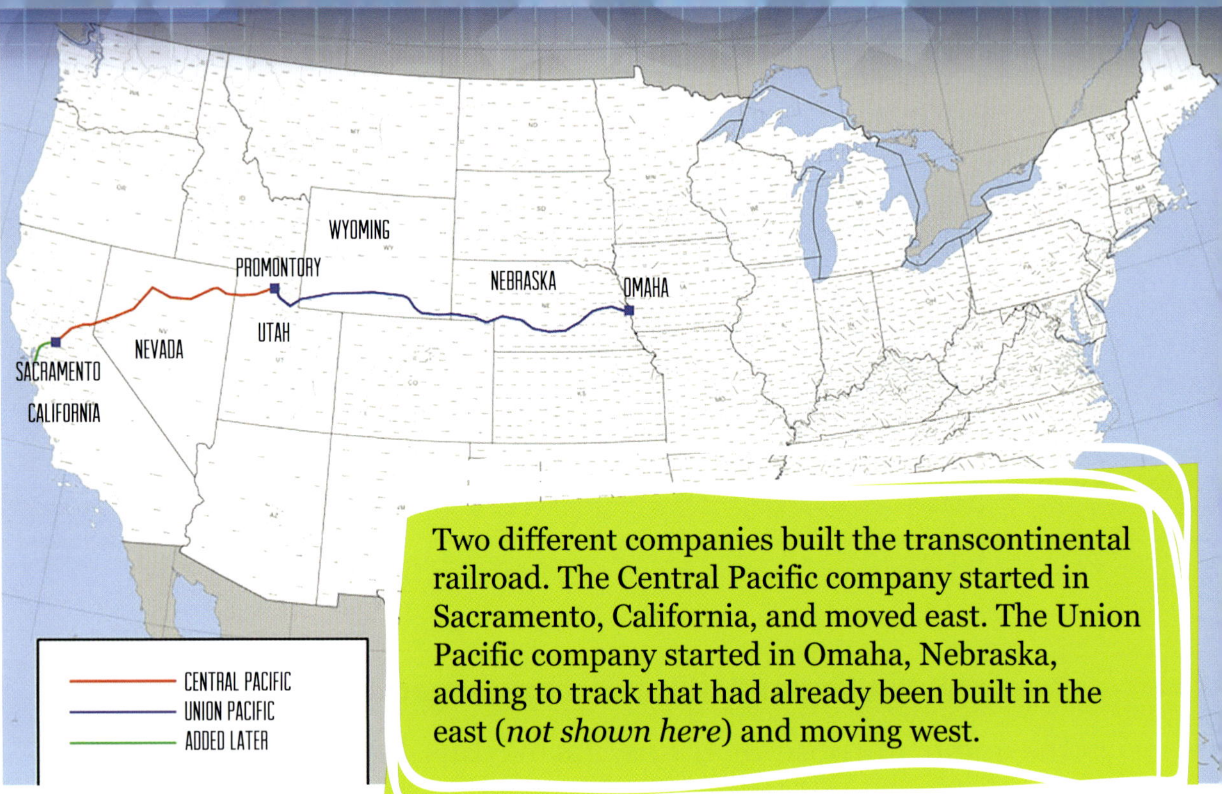


Two different companies built the transcontinental railroad. The Central Pacific company started in Sacramento, California, and moved east. The Union Pacific company started in Omaha, Nebraska, adding to track that had already been built in the east (*not shown here*) and moving west.

They transported guns, ammunition, and troops in wars. They brought food and supplies over mountains and rivers.

One limitation of trains is that they can only go where there are tracks, so tracks had to be built. On May 10, 1869, Leland Stanford drove the last spike into a rail at Promontory Point in the Utah territory to join the rails of the first transcontinental railroad. The transcontinental railroad allowed goods and passengers to travel across the United States more easily. In the past, goods going from one coast to the other had to travel on ships all the way around Cape Horn, at the southern tip of South America. The 15,000-mile (24,140 km) trip took between three and six months. It was a very dangerous journey. Train travel was safer and faster, which also made it less expensive.

Trains also carried people. When people first started riding on trains, they either sat in open-air cars on wooden benches or they stood. Sometimes, sparks from wood-fired and coal-fired boilers landed on passengers' clothing and set them on fire. Soot and smoke caused coughing and eye pain. These issues had to be addressed before train travel could become safe and comfortable.

George Pullman formed a company in 1862 to take care of this problem. He designed passenger cars that were more comfortable. For example, seats could be made into beds for long trips.

This drawing from the 1870s shows the inside of a Pullman car. Today, train cars are more often filled with many seats that are very close together.

## LOOKING AT STEAM ENGINES

Although Robert Trevithick was the first to invent the locomotive steam engine, he had a hard time selling it, and he did not want to make any changes to it.

Other inventors stepped in to make those changes. One of the most important was a man named George Stephenson. In 1825, he engineered his first steam locomotive to be used on a public railway system. This invention took a plentiful source of fuel, such as coal or wood, and turned it into mechanical energy.

Mechanical energy is the ability of something to work or to move. This meant the steam locomotive could do the work of many men. Steam locomotives could also move much more weight much more quickly than a horse-drawn cart. More coal could be mined and hauled to the sea. Factories far away from the mines could then have more coal to fuel their machines.

Early steam locomotives were complicated machines. They burned wood or coal in a fireproof box. This firebox had pipes

This diagram shows how one kind of steam engine works.

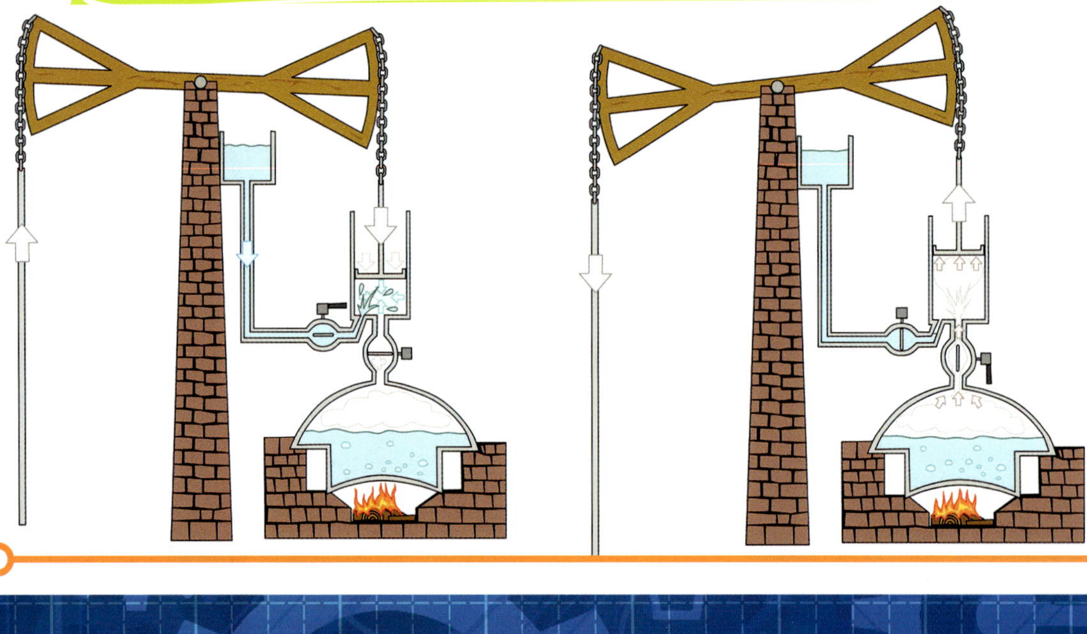

that extended into a large container called a boiler, which was filled with water. When the pipes got hot, so did the water in the boiler. When the water was hot enough, it turned into steam.

Think about what happens in a water gun. The water goes into a large cylinder but does not have any power until it goes into a small tube and is squeezed out under pressure through a small opening. The same thing happens with the steam in a locomotive.

The water in the boiler was superheated to more than 212 degrees Fahrenheit (100 degrees Celsius). When a liquid turns into a gas, such as water turning to steam, it expands. As the steam expanded, it moved into a smaller steam pipe that led into a cylinder. In the cylinder was a moving part called a piston, which was connected to a straight rod. The straight rod was connected to a wheel. As the steam flooded into the cylinder under pressure, it pushed the piston back and forth. This moved the rod and turned the wheel, moving the train.

The steam engine worked well, but it had problems. For example, the engine was very heavy because it was made of iron. In the early years, its weight often broke the iron rails of the tracks. Engineers solved this by adding more wheels to the locomotive. This distributed the weight more evenly over the whole length of the locomotive.

Sometimes the firebox in the locomotive got so hot that it exploded, injuring or killing anyone who was in the area. This was dangerous not only for the engineer driving the train, but also for the passengers. If the engineer was dead or too hurt to control the train, it was likely to **derail**. Inventors solved this problem by inserting a lead plug at the top of the firebox. If the box got too hot, the plug would melt and warn the attendant so he could stop it from exploding.

## A NEW KIND OF ENGINE

Steam locomotives were very popular until the 1930s. Around that time, people started to realize that they needed to improve train engines. Steam engines cost a lot to operate, and they were powered by coal, which is very harmful to the environment. Gasoline and oil were used in locomotives for a while, but these also had problems: Oil-powered locomotives were not powerful enough to pull heavy loads, and gas engines were not any cheaper to operate.

A man named Rudolph Diesel invented a new engine, powered by a new kind of fuel, in 1892. Both the engine and the fuel are called diesel after him. Diesel releases more energy when it is burned than gasoline does, so a diesel engine is more **efficient** and requires less fuel. Engineers started

## An Idea That Never Took Off

When nuclear power was discovered, some engineers thought it could be an exciting new way to power locomotives. In the 1950s, Dr. Lyle B. Borst and his students came up with a solution to train travel's fuel issues: nuclear-powered trains. The plan was to put a small nuclear reactor on the train to power electric motors that would turn the wheels. Radiation can be deadly, so to protect the passengers, the reactor would be enclosed in a lead shield that weighed 200 tons (181 metric tons). The train, which was named the X-12, seemed like a great idea at first. Nuclear power does not put out dangerous **emissions** the way fossil fuels do, and it lasts so much longer than other types of fuel that the train would have been able to run for months without needing to be refueled.

Although Borst was given a **patent** for his design, the X-12 was never made. It would have been expensive, and new information was coming to light in the 1950s about the dangers of nuclear reactors. For example, if the lead shield broke in any way—such as if the train was in an accident—the radiation could leak out and hurt or kill the passengers.

experimenting with a combination of diesel fuel and electric power in locomotive engines. Heavy freight loads could be pulled using a diesel-electric engine with less pollution and cost. By the 1940s, this type of engine was the standard for new trains.

Steam engines are external combustion engines. That means that the combustion, or burning of the fuel, happens outside the engine. The burning fuel heats a tube, which then gives the heat to the water inside the boiler. This is called a heat exchange.

Diesel engines are internal combustion engines, so the fuel is heated inside the engine. This makes internal combustion engines more powerful and efficient. They have fewer mechanical parts than steam engines, so they are lighter and do not break as easily. Diesel locomotives use less fuel and haul heavier loads, so they are less expensive to operate.

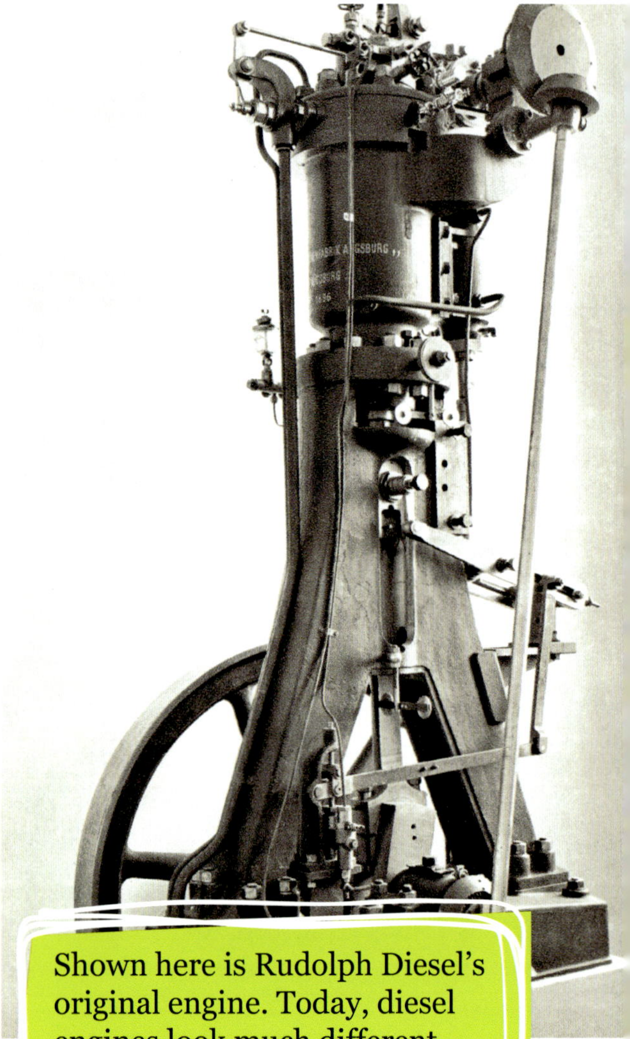

Shown here is Rudolph Diesel's original engine. Today, diesel engines look much different.

Internal combustion engines have cylinders in them. Each cylinder has a moving part called a piston attached to it. Valves on the cylinder let fuel in and emissions out. As an engine runs, it goes through several strokes, or phases. Most diesel engines have four strokes: intake, compression, combustion, and exhaustion. On the intake stroke, the valve at the top opens to let air into the cylinder.

On the compression stroke, the valve closes, and the piston moves to the top. As it goes up, its movement compresses, or squeezes, the air into a small space. As the air is compressed, it gets very hot. On the combustion stroke, the fuel is injected into the cylinder full of hot, compressed air. This causes a small explosion that pushes the piston back down. On the exhaust stroke, a different valve opens, and the piston rises up again to push out the exhaust from the burned fuel. The parts of the engine are connected, so the piston's movement causes the rest of the parts of the engine to move.

The diesel engine was a huge advancement in train technology. The fuel generally costs less. Also, the engine is more efficient, so it can run for longer on less fuel. However, diesel pollutes the air even more than gasoline does. Air pollution is a leading cause of climate change, so experts are looking for ways to make trains more eco-friendly, or better for the environment.

## THINK IT THROUGH

1. Why do you think trains have multiple cars?
2. What are some other problems a nuclear-powered train might have beyond those mentioned here?
3. Which development in early train technology do you think was the most important, and why?

Many people in the United States enjoy taking road trips, but high-speed trains would be able to move people across the country much faster than cars.

CHAPTER TWO

# Faster Than Ever

Around the 1970s, cars became much more common, especially in the United States. The size of the country makes it difficult to get around by train. Cars can go places trains cannot because of a lack of rail tracks. In Europe, trains are more popular, but not as much as they were before cars became common. Airplane travel has also contributed to the decline in trains' popularity. However, trains are still a good way to move goods around. Engineers are also working on ways to make trains fast enough to compete with planes.

## USING ELECTRICITY

Today, most people think of electric vehicles as futuristic. However, people have been experimenting with electric vehicles for hundreds of years. In 1837, a Scottish chemist named Robert Davidson built an electric locomotive **prototype** that was only big enough to carry two people. Between 1840 and

Robert Davidson (*shown here*) made amazing advancements in electric train technology.

1842, he brought it to several exhibitions. Davidson also built a full-size prototype electric locomotive and tested it on a public railway in 1842. However, an unknown person or group of people destroyed it before it could make its way back to Davidson. He suspected the criminals were people who did not want to see steam trains replaced. However, they likely did not have to worry, since Davidson could not find anyone to pay for the research that would make his electric engine a success. In the 1840s, battery technology was not advanced enough to run large trains. Davidson's batteries were very expensive to make, and they could not be recharged the way most batteries today, such as phone batteries, can.

The idea of using electricity to power trains was not completely abandoned, though. In 1879, the electric lightbulb was invented. It demonstrated how clean and inexpensive electricity could be, and cities started putting in electric grids to power houses and businesses. Engineers realized that trains could be hooked up to the grid too. This was achieved either through an overhead line or an electrified third rail, depending on where the train's route ran.

Eventually, many new kinds of trains were developed. Cable cars ran on streets in San Francisco, California. These cars hung from a single rail and were powered by electricity. Subways took trains underground. Electric-powered streetcars ran on rails and connected neighborhoods in large cities. Interurban railways took passengers from one town to another. All of this was done without the soot, sparks, and dangerous emissions steam and diesel locomotives produced.

## A FUTURISTIC WAY TO TRAVEL

Superfast trains might sound like something out of science fiction, but they have existed for decades. Most high-speed rail (HSR) trains have between 8 and 16 cars that are permanently hooked together. This group of cars is called a train set. At the front of the train set is the locomotive. It is generally powered by an electric line. HSR trains go faster if they travel on a flat, straight track. Rail routes with fewer curves allow trains to stay at higher speeds for the longest amount of time.

## Using Renewable Energy

The climate change crisis has made people look for ways to reduce emissions from all kinds of transportation, including trains. One way to do this might be to use the power of the sun to generate electricity. Several countries, such as the United Kingdom (UK), India, and Australia, are working on solar-powered trains and train lines. This is generally done by putting solar panels on the trains or near the tracks.

However, there are some concerns about switching to solar power completely. For one thing, solar panels only work on very sunny days. This is less of a problem in India and Australia than it is in the UK, which has a lot of rainy and sometimes snowy days. For the trains to run on these days, the power needs to be stored in batteries. However, these batteries are expensive. Furthermore, getting the materials needed to make them can be harmful for the environment. Most batteries use a metal called lithium, which needs to be mined. Digging the mines can pollute water and harm wildlife. Experts are currently working on developing batteries that use different materials.

There is no real definition for a high-speed rail system. Any train that can travel above 90 miles (145 km) per hour is considered an HSR. Today, some trains are physically able to travel at speeds up to 220 miles (322 km) per hour. However, in reality, they generally travel much more slowly. Physical laws and track **infrastructure** limit how fast trains can go. The angle of curves, time needed to stop a train or signal to cars and other trains, and passenger comfort and safety must be considered as trains are made to go faster. For instance, an Amtrak train called the Acela has a top speed of 220 miles (322 km) per hour, but on the route it runs, it is only allowed to go 66 miles (106 km) per hour most of the time.

A network of HSR tracks can take passengers all across Europe. Shown here is an HSR train (*right*) alongside a highway (*left*) near Madrid, Spain.

Other countries are far ahead of the United States in HSR development. Japan was one of the first to upgrade its train system when the country introduced its “bullet trains” in 1964. They are called this because the locomotive’s small, round nose makes it look like a bullet. This design helps lessen wind resistance, which makes them able to travel up to 200 miles (320 km) per hour. Japan is proud to say that as of early 2022, the bullet trains have not had a single passenger death or injury due to train accidents.

Europe was next to upgrade its trains. France started in 1981, and other European countries soon followed. Today, an HSR network crisscrosses the continent, moving passengers within and between countries. These trains can significantly

Bullet trains such as the one shown here have a long, flat nose that makes them easy to identify.

cut down on travel time. For example, traveling from Rome to Milan in Italy takes 9 hours on a standard train, but only 3 hours on an HSR train.

China came later to the HSR game, but it made up for the delay with amazing technology. In the 1990s, China started planning for a system that was modeled on Japan's. In 2008, the first HSR line opened in China. These trains can go up to 217 miles (350 km) per hour, making them the fastest in the world as of late 2021. China has also rapidly expanded its HSR system. By 2025, the country expects to have more than 24,000 miles (38,000 km) of HSR track. China's HSR system is so efficient that many airlines have completely stopped flying some of their shorter routes within the country.

Compared to other countries, the United States is lagging far behind. One reason for this is that cities are not putting in the money needed to improve train infrastructure. Another is that Europe and Asia have a lot of people living close together, while the United States has a lot of small towns scattered widely throughout the country. Additionally, the distance between major U.S. cities is generally much farther than it is in other countries. Connecting all these towns and cities to an HSR system would be very difficult and expensive. Americans are also very emotionally attached to their cars. There is a large network of roads throughout the United States, and many people enjoy the freedom a car gives. Finally, there is political opposition to trains from companies that sell fossil fuels used in cars. These companies can lobby, or ask, the government not to work on improving train lines, and they can also make advertisements that convince people cars are better than trains.

## MAGLEV TRAINS

Magnetic **levitation**, or maglev, trains use magnets to create a force called electromagnetic induction. This moves the train instead of an engine. All magnets have a north pole and a south pole. Like poles repel, while opposite poles attract. With electromagnetic induction, electricity is generated in metal coils when the two poles of the magnets rotate from repelling each other to attracting each other.

Maglev trains can move at incredible speeds.

To make the trains move, supermagnetized coils are attached on the inside of the outer rails. Large magnets are attached to the underside of the train. As the magnets repel and attract each other, the train floats above the track and moves. Maglev trains slow down and stop by moving the magnets closer to or farther away from the track. Maglev trains have no wheels touching the track, so there is no friction slowing them down. This allows the trains to travel even faster than HSR trains. Maglev trains have reached speeds of more than 310 miles (499 km) per hour. In 2016, a Japanese maglev train reached 374 miles (601 km) per hour. For comparison, an airplane can fly at a speed of about 562 miles (904.5 km) per hour.

Removing friction also makes trains quieter and less shaky. Furthermore, since there is no engine, the train does not release polluting emissions. All of these factors help reduce traffic, noise, and pollution in large cities.

## THINK IT THROUGH

1. Do you think HSR systems will ever become common in the United States the way they are in other countries?
2. Why do HSR trains work better on straight tracks?
3. Why doesn't every city have a maglev train system?

Shown here is a model of an early passenger train car. Even after Pullman cars became common, these wooden benches could still be found in third-class carriages, which was all some travelers could afford.

CHAPTER THREE

# Design Challenges

Although 21st-century trains can travel at amazing speeds, the people who design them must always keep in mind that they are meant to carry people and goods. Having a train shoot down a track at nearly the speed of an airplane and come to a sudden stop would cause anything—or anyone—inside to be thrown forward. Train designers also need to think about things such as how the tracks work with the train, how to make passengers comfortable, and how to make freight cars easy for people to load and unload.

## CARS FOR PEOPLE

On early train trips, passengers stood on an open-air, wooden platform covered only by a roof. Small holes in the floor drained rainwater. Eventually, enclosed wooden benches that held six people were installed. These were uncomfortable to sit on for a long time and were often too crowded.

Some early steam trains simply attached a group of stagecoaches together. Flanged wheels that fit on the metal tracks replaced the regular wheels. That is why passenger cars are sometimes called coaches or carriages, even today. Some countries call a train car frame a bogie. The wheels and support for the train car are attached to this frame.

Trains with steam engines and wooden cars were not only uncomfortable but also not very safe. They would break apart or catch on fire easily if the train derailed.

Shown here is the dining car on a luxury train.

Today, passenger cars are made of steel, are enclosed, and have padded seats. They are also equipped with air-conditioning and bathrooms. Special cars are available where travelers can eat, sleep, or view the countryside. Some luxury trains have even been designed to look more like hotels than trains. They may include stained glass windows, comfortable couches instead of train seats, and large cabins with private bathrooms. The bogies on all trains today have shock absorbers attached to them and better couplings to help absorb the movement of the cars so the ride is more comfortable.

## CARS FOR OBJECTS

Freight car designs have changed as the kind of freight they carry has changed. Businesses that use trains to move their freight are concerned about cost. Engineers work to design freight cars that are both strong and light, since this saves money; heavy loads move slower and use more fuel.

Even with a light design, train cars get very heavy once they are loaded up with things such as coal, logs, sand, or wheat. Locomotives must be powerful enough to pull heavy loads up hills. They also have to be able to stop quickly and safely. Since a train car full of freight is heavier than one full of people, the

## Alfred Ely Beach's Subway

In the mid-1800s, New York City was growing incredibly crowded. People suggested all kinds of ways to get traffic off the streets, such as an elevated train or moving walkway. Alfred Ely Beach suggested an underground system, but he got almost no support for this idea. People were worried that digging under such a large city would cause it to collapse. However, Beach decided to build it in secret and show everyone later that it was a good idea.

Beach received a permit to build a **pneumatic** tube system that would send letters to and from the post office. However, he actually built his tube big enough to carry passengers. He and his crew worked at night, taking away the dirt in quiet carts so no one would be able to tell how big he was making the tunnel. In 1870, he gave demonstrations of his subway system, which was powered by a giant fan. The fan would blow the car forward, and when it was time to stop or reverse direction, a man would flip a switch to reverse the flow of the fan, sucking the car back. Beach received permission to expand throughout the city, but a combination of political opposition and an economic recession stopped him from following through with this first subway system.

train's brakes, car bodies, and couplers must be stronger than those of passenger cars.

Early freight cars were made of wood, then changed to iron, then to steel. Steel is strong, light, and durable. Originally, cars were designed with sides but without roofs. In some countries, this style is still used. For example, Mauritania has only one train line. All the cars are open on top. Passengers can pay to sit in the last car on the train, but since this car is exactly like all the others, many people choose the free option: sitting on top of the freight in the other cars. It is a dusty ride through the desert that is very hot during the day and very cold at night. Most trains in other parts of the world use covered cars to protect freight—and people—from the weather.

## A CRUCIAL PART

Without tracks, trains cannot run, so track design is just as important as the design of the train itself. Early wooden rails wore out quickly. Iron straps placed on top of the rails made

Shown here are Mauritanian people and goats riding on top of freight cars filled with iron ore.

them last longer, but engineers discovered that heavy freight cars broke the iron straps. When steel was created, engineers found that steel rails could be rolled out in large sheets. Also, steel was smooth and easy to shape. Train wheels rolled over steel tracks with less resistance, letting trains travel faster.

As more tracks were laid, engineers encountered unique problems with curves. They found that if tracks were laid with one rail higher than the other on curves, it counteracted **centrifugal force**. Braking at the right speed while going around curves also kept the train from derailing.

A train can only switch tracks when both tracks are the same gauge. This is why most tracks today are standardized.

**Gauges** varied due to the differing widths of carts and bogies. Engineers worked to find which gauge was best. Smaller-gauge tracks were less expensive to build, but to use them, trains had to travel slower and be lighter. Wider gauges allowed trains to get up to higher speeds and carry heavier loads, but they cost more to lay down. Additionally, switching between gauges meant passengers and freight needed to be transferred to different trains to get to certain destinations. Currently, most railways are now standardized at a gauge of 4 feet, 8.5 inches (1.42 meters).

## COUPLING THE CARS

Early train cars were coupled together by chains and had no brakes on the individual cars. When the horses or locomotive stopped the train, all the cars would bump together. Since early trains did not travel very quickly, no one got hurt, but it was uncomfortable. However, if a car became uncoupled from the train for any reason, it could not be stopped or even held in place. After this realization, engineers started putting brakes on every car.

As trains hauled heavier loads and moved at faster speeds, stopping safely and quickly became more important. As a train stops, it needs to release energy. Engineers need to know how much pressure to apply to the wheels and when to start applying that pressure so the train stops safely. If brakes are applied too quickly and with too much pressure, the train can derail; too slowly, and it can crash into obstacles such as other trains or animals that have wandered onto the tracks. A train that stops too slowly can also pass its stop completely, forcing passengers to walk back to the station.

Brakes greatly improved with electricity. A man named George Westinghouse designed an air brake that used electricity

Shown here is a knuckle coupler.

to send compressed air evenly to the brakes, causing all the wheels on all the cars to stop at the same time. By 1880, his brake design was the standard on most trains. It is still in use today.

By the mid-1800s, brakes were not the only thing that had improved. Instead of chains, trains now had couplers that connected cars with a stiff pin and loop. These kept the cars from bumping together, but they were dangerous. Many injuries occurred when trains backed up and cars slammed together while workers were trying to connect them. During the American Civil War (1861–1865), a man named Eli Janney realized there was a safer way to couple cars together. His coupler looks like two hands clasped together is and secured with an automatic pin in the middle. It is called a knuckle coupler, and he received a patent for it in 1873. Modern trains still use thc basic dcsign of the knuckle coupler, but people have improved it to keep cars from coming apart when a train derails.

## THINK IT THROUGH

1. Why are wooden cars less safe than steel?
2. Why does laying one rail higher than the other counteract centrifugal force?
3. Why is it important for all of a train's wheels to stop at the same time?

Train tracks that are not well maintained, such as those shown here, pose a serious danger. Electric sensors are a feature that can let drivers know about broken rails.

CHAPTER FOUR

# Looking Ahead

Although cars and airplanes are more popular forms of transportation in the United States, trains—especially freight trains—are still a very important part of the economy. In the 21st century, engineers continue to look for ways to improve trains by making them faster, safer, more efficient, more comfortable, and more eco-friendly, or green.

## GREENER AND SAFER

As people look for a solution to the climate change crisis, some have proposed hydrogen-powered trains. These trains would use fuel cells instead of electricity. A chemical reaction happens inside the fuel cell when hydrogen and oxygen are mixed together. This reaction creates energy and sends it to the batteries, which then power the engine. Unlike diesel trains, locomotives that use hydrogen fuel produce only steam and water, and the engine is very quiet.

Another issue engineers are working on is how to make trains safer. Trains are already a very safe way to travel, but accidents still happen. Some companies are looking at electronic sensors to improve safety. A company called Siemens has developed a broken rail detection (BRD) system. A broken rail is very dangerous, but drivers often have no way of knowing about it until they see it. By then, it is often too late to stop the train. The BRD system helps prevent derailments by sending them the location of broken rails ahead of time.

Another way to keep trains safe is by using drones to monitor the tracks. These unmanned aircraft could fly ahead of the train and send back information about any unexpected obstacle on the tracks, including animals, fallen branches, cars or people.

## FASTER AND MORE EFFICIENT

Even though HSR trains already exist, people are working on making trains even faster. Elon Musk proposed an idea in 2013 that he called the hyperloop. A hyperloop does not have connected cars the way a regular train does. Instead, it works by sending passenger pods through a large tube. A combination of pneumatic and magnetic technology could allow the pods to travel at top speeds of 700 miles (1,126 km) per hour.

However, as of 2021, the fastest a hyperloop train has traveled is 288 miles (463 km) per hour. This record was set by a German company called TUM Hyperloop. The main reason for this is that not enough hyperloop track has been built yet to allow these trains to reach their top speed; the trip is over before they can get up to that level.

Others are working on making maglev trains faster than ever. However, there are concerns that in their quest for speed, some people are disregarding safety. For example, China put a speed limit on its trains in 2017, six years after a crash killed 38 people and injured 192 more. However, China is also working on a maglev train that could go as fast as a hyperloop. Some experts are concerned that not every safety problem will be addressed before this train is put into service.

Aside from making trains run faster, another way to decrease the amount of time a train trip takes is to maximize efficiency. For instance, subways are often crowded, especially in cities such as New York City and Tokyo.

This picture shows what a hyperloop train and track might look like. The track is actually a large tube, not the regular train tracks that have been used for centuries.

## Underwater and in the Air

The idea of an underwater train might seem bizarre, but several already exist. The most famous is the Channel Tunnel, nicknamed the "Chunnel," that connects London and Paris underneath the English Channel. A similar project is underway in India. However, the most ambitious is China's plan to build an HSR system that stretches for more than 8,000 miles (13,000 km) through Russia, underwater to Alaska, over the Yukon mountains of Canada, and into the United States. As of 2021, China is working on its plan, but no track has been laid yet.

Another unusual train proposal is the Link & Fly train by AKKA Technologies. This is a train/plane **hybrid** with a **fuselage** that could detach from the plane and attach to a train as a carriage. However, people are not stopping at the sky. There are also plans for a train to outer space! The Startram would use maglev technology to run along a track that rises 1,000 miles (1,609 km) into the air. It would accelerate along the way, eventually getting fast enough to shoot off the track and into low Earth orbit. As of 2021, the Startram is only an idea, but people hope it will one day become reality.

Waiting for a car with enough room in it can take up a large part of a person's travel time. To address this, a company called PriestmanGoode came up with an idea for seats that fold and unfold to make room for more people in each car. Waiting in a line to pay for the train ride and get through a **turnstile** can also add time on to a trip. A company called Cubic Transportation Systems is working to address this with a system that uses facial recognition to scan people's faces and electronically charge them for their ticket. However, many people worry that facial recognition software could be dangerous, so this is not a popular option even though it is more efficient.

Folding seats such as the ones on this Finnish train could help make space for more people in each car.

A third way to increase the efficiency of train trips is to reduce the number of stops. However, this limits the places where people can get on and off trains. To address both these issues, PriestmanGoode came up with another idea. This one involves a city train that travels alongside an HSR train and links up to it so people can transfer from one to the other without either train having to stop. This idea has some very serious safety issues to work out before it can become reality, but the idea is appealing to many people. There is no shortage of ideas for improving train travel in the future; the only limitation is the current technology.

## THINK IT THROUGH

1. Why do you think hydrogen trains are not common yet?
2. What kinds of safety problems need to be worked out before people can make even faster trains?
3. Can you think of other ways to make train travel more efficient?

# GLOSSARY

**centrifugal force:** A force on an object moving in a circular path that makes the object move out and away from its center.

**derail:** To leave the tracks.

**efficient:** Able to produce a desired result with little waste.

**emissions:** Anything, such as a gas or steam, that is released out into the open.

**flanged wheel:** A wheel with a rimmed edge that keeps it on a rail.

**fuselage:** The main body of an airplane.

**gauge:** The width from the inside edge of one rail to the other.

**hybrid:** An object that is a combination of two or more different things.

**infrastructure:** The basic equipment and structures that are needed for a country, region, or organization to function properly.

**levitation:** The act of suspending an object in the air.

**patent:** A document that gives the inventor the right to be the only one to make or sell the invention for a certain number of years.

**pneumatic:** Using air pressure to move or work.

**prototype:** An original or first model of something from which other forms are copied.

**turnstile:** A gate at an entrance that has turning arms and allows only one person at a time to go through.

# FIND OUT MORE

## Books

Hancock, James Gulliver. *Trains*. Dublin, Ireland: Lonely Planet, 2020.

Meister, Cari. *Trains*. Oxford, UK: Raintree, 2020.

West, David. *What's Inside Trains*. London, UK: Franklin Watts, 2018.

## Websites

**BrainPOP: Railroad History**
*www.brainpop.com/technology/transportation/railroadhistory*
Learn about how trains evolved over time.

**DK Find Out!: History of Trains**
*www.dkfindout.com/us/transportation/history-trains*
This interactive website includes information about the history of trains as well as pictures of various train designs.

**Kids Discover: Trains**
*online.kidsdiscover.com/unit/trains*
Read about how trains have changed the world and do activities such as crossword puzzles.

## Organizations

**Southern California Railway Museum**
2201 South A Street
Perris, CA 92570
Email: info@socalrailway.org
*socalrailway.org*
This museum houses a collection of real train cars and locomotives, along with a railway where visitors can ride some of these historic trains. At Christmas, the museum hosts a special Polar Express ride, complete with cookies and hot chocolate, dancing chefs, and a meet-and-greet with Santa.

**Train Collectors Association**
300 Paradise Lane
Ronks, PA 17572
*www.tcatrains.org*
The Train Collectors Association connects people who have a love of toy trains. The association also has a museum, located at the address above.

**Publisher's note to educators and parents:** Our editors have carefully reviewed these websites to ensure that they are suitable for students. Many websites change frequently, however, and we cannot guarantee that a site's future contents will continue to meet our high standards of quality and educational value. Be advised that students should be closely supervised whenever they access the Internet.

# INDEX

# ABOUT THE AUTHOR

**SOPHIE WASHBURNE** has been a freelance writer and editor of young adult and adult books for more than 10 years. She travels extensively with her husband, Alan. When they are not traveling, they live in Wales with their cat, Zoe. Sophie enjoys doing crafts and cooking when she has spare time.